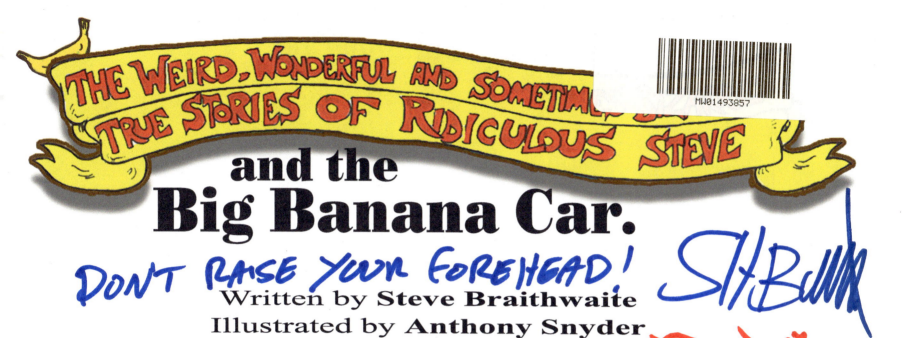

THE WEIRD, WONDERFUL AND SOMETIMES TRUE STORIES OF RIDICULOUS STEVE

and the
Big Banana Car.

Don't raise your forehead!

Written by **Steve Braithwaite**

Illustrated by **Anthony Snyder**

Partially edited by **Teresa Phillips**

Published by
Mutant Publishing

Produced by

Money Grubbing Productions *

A division of

Capitalist Pig Enterprises **

Which is a wholly owned subsidiary of

The Worldwide, Global Indentured Servitude Corporation ***

Printed by McNaughton and Gunn, Michigan, USA.

First edition 2020
25 24 23 22 21 20 | 7 6 5 4 3 2 1
ISBN: .978-1-7350669-0-5

* Doesn't exist   ** Also doesn't exist   *** Really, really doesn't exist.

The Big Banana Car
Ambassador-At-Large
Program

I would like to thank **Teresa Phillips** for nominating

her many nephews and nieces to the position of

Big Banana Car Roving Ambassadors-at-Large.

This is largely a ceremonial position and comes without portfolio,

but it does mean that you can make your own ambassadors sash and

regale the other children at school with stories about the Big Banana Car

that you either personally experienced or read about online.

Teresa writes:

"To all my beloved Littles with whom I've read

countless books. May we continue to giggle together!"

This book has hidden secrets.

Even though this is a book about bananas there are many other delicious fruits and vegetables and so we have hidden some in the drawings. See if you can find them.

1) 21 Pineapples
(of different sizes)

2) 12 Sweet Corn

3) 7 Apples

4) 4 Pea Pods

5) 8 Pears

6) 4 Watermelons

7) 2 Bunches of Grapes

8) 9 Carots

9) 8 Oranges

and on to the story .....

There once was a man.

Some would say a rather unusual man.

He wouldn't say that though.

He would say he was the most normal man in the world and that everyone else was sort of weird.

But that's not entirely true.

He's the weirdo.

But he's a nice weirdo.

In this story we'll call him Steve.

Because that's his name.

Steve.

He calls himself Magnificent Steve.

But we're not going to do that.

Not at all!

To us he's just plain Steve.

Or maybe even Ridiculous Steve.

One day Ridiculous Steve had an idea.

He closed his eyes and pictured a giant

banana driving down the road and with that

one simple thought, he started laughing.

"I know" he said to himself,

"I'll build a car that looks like a huge banana"

Because, why not?

And for Ridiculous Steve nothing was

more important than laughing.

Except for brushing your teeth.

That was important.

And wearing clothes.

That was also pretty important.

Except in bed. That would be silly.

Unless they were pajamas.

Then it would be okay.

So that's what Ridiculous Steve did. He gathered together some friends, and they decided to build a car that looked like a banana. They cut up pieces of metal and all started laughing because they were building a big banana car. They welded the pieces of metal together to look like a banana and kept on laughing.

Then one day they put the big pretend banana on top of an old truck and guess what? They looked at it and smiled at each other and then continued right on laughing.

They drove the Big Banana Car
all around town and all the people
who saw them started laughing too.

19

They drove down the highway
and people in the other cars saw them
and started laughing.

They drove past farms
and fields and meadows,

and the cows and chickens saw

them and started laughing.

Some people just smiled and

gave Steve a big thumbs up.

23

Steve drove his Banana Car
up and down and all around.

He drove it here, he drove it there,
he drove it almost everywhere.

Ridiculous Steve was driving the banana car in the mountains one day when a policeman stopped him. The policeman said to Steve in a very stern voice "The reason I pulled you over is because at that light back there you peeled out." Steve looked at the policeman, and the policeman looked at Steve. And Steve looked at the policeman some more and the policeman looked back at Steve. And then they both burst out laughing.

Steve drove fast, he drove slow,

he drove wherever he could go.

He drove east, he drove west,

he then drove to a music fest.

One day while Steve was driving in his Big Banana Car he met a lady who had been sad for a very long time. She told Steve that she had cried everyday for a whole week, but when she saw the Big Banana Car she smiled, and that made Steve happy.

She then invited Steve and his Big Banana Car to her music festival, and because Steve likes to dance he went and they all were dancing and laughing.

31

Steve drove through rain,

he drove through snow,

he drove where many tourists go.

He drove past beaches,

and tall palm trees,

he drove to the tip of the Florida Keys.

In Key West Ridiculous Steve met an astronaut who wore his glasses upside down and when he saw the Big Banana Car he couldn't stop laughing.

He laughed and laughed and when he was finally done laughing he told Steve that he was having an astronaut party at the place where they launch the space rockets and he invited Steve and the Big Banana Car.

And then he laughed some more.

He drove past ponds

and drove past trees,

he drove past goats and honey bees.

He drove on grass

he drove through mud

and one day saw a giant spud.

Ridiculous Steve was invited to a school to show the children the Big Banana Car and while he was there a huge potato on the back of a truck stopped by.

The potato was owned by some clever people in Idaho who knew if kids laughed when they saw a giant spud they just might eat more potatoes.

It was so big that Steve could stand up inside it.

Steve drove past lakes

and over streams,

he drove by fields with soccer teams.

He drove it north,

he drove it south,

he drove into a lions mouth.

He didn't really drive into a lions mouth.
That was the only thing Steve could think of that rhymes with south.

One day the Big Banana Car was driving in Hollywood, California.

It was a bright and sunny day and some famous TV people saw the car and asked "Can we drive in your banana car?"

And so they did and it was on television.

He drove it up,

he drove it down,

he drove it all around the town.

He drove it high,

he drove it low,

he drove it to an art car show.

Some lovely people in Texas heard about Ridiculous Steve and his Big Banana Car and said, "We have a parade every year with lots of crazy cars and we want you to join us."

So Steve drove his banana car to Houston and met lots of new friends who all drive weird and wonderful cars, and Steve didn't feel so strange anymore.

He drove to Canada, and Mexico,

he crossed tall bridges

with rivers below.

He drove beneath

the winter skies

and one day had a nice surprise.

HOLLYWOOD

I ♥ NY

49

One chilly November morning Steve decided it was to cold to drive a banana car in Michigan and so he left for the warm weather of Texas. Along the way an eagle eyed State Trooper spotted Steve and asked if he could take a look at his unusual car.

When they were done chatting and it was time for Steve to go, the police officer surprised Steve by giving him $20 for gas and wished him "Safe travels".

He drove all day,

he drove all night,

he drove beneath the bright moonlight.

He drove on roads,

and on the street,

he drove on sand in burning heat.

Some crazy fun people have a big art festival in the desert every year, and they all drive weird cars like Steve's.

They asked if he would like to join them, so he did. And Steve realized that it was okay to build weird things and even drive them around.

And now everywhere Ridiculous Steve goes he meets strange weird people driving strange weird cars and they are now his family.

Can you Spot the 14 differences between these two banana car pictures?

58

To find the answers and play more Spot the Difference games visit BigBananaCar.com and go to the **Fun** page.

59

How many bananas are in this book?

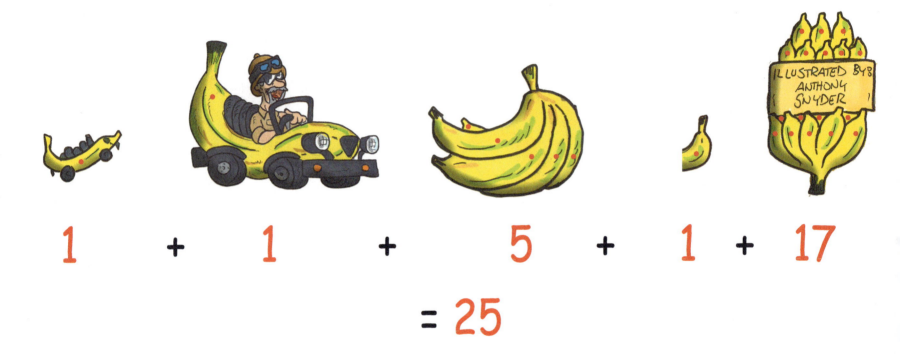

1 + 1 + 5 + 1 + 17

= 25

Are you good at counting?

Some might be tricky when they're in a bunch.

The answer is at BigBananaCar.com.

Oh no, we've lost Anthony!!

The pictures in this book were drawn by Anthony Snyder and he
enjoyed it so much he's decided to hide in one of them.

See if you can find him.

The original Banana Car build crew

Ron Kutt.

I had a very important steering component that needed to be welded and the welding machine I was using wasn't powerful enough. Ron is the owner of a mobile welding company and so I called him in. Apart from being a very skilled fabricator Ron is also a car guy and was very helpful with many aspects of the banana car build. He ended up working on the project until it's completion.

Liz O'Neill.

Liz was amazing. She took to the project straight away and wanted to help in any way she could. She offered her large workshop for the build and had many great ideas and input.

Steve Myers.

Steve was instrumental in getting the Big Banana Car project off the ground and moving it forward.

He owns his own internet radio station at FlintTalk.com along with many other websites.

Mark Steele.

Auto body craftsman and general automotive expert.
Mark has his own body shop in Bowling Green, Ohio. He has an astounding knowledge of all things automotive and the skills needed to repair and restore vintage automobiles. The banana car project was started at Marks Bowling Green location and with his help progressed very quickly.

Glen Lewis.

Glen is not only a very skilled auto mechanic but he is someone who doesn't need much direction. Give him the basic outline of a job and he goes non stop, working quietly until suddenly you look over and it's finished.

Rick Willens.

Rick first saw the Big Banana Car in a news article and thought, "This is something, I'd like to be a part of" He volunteered his airbrushing talents and introduced me to Jim Lacey of J&L Auto Body who painted the base coat. Rick then got to "work his magic" and airbrushed the banana car to look just Like a REAL Banana. The Airbrushing took about 5 hours and I must say that Rick did an excellent job! The most common comment I have heard since he airbrushed it is "Wow, it really does look like a banana with the green fading"

The banana car has taken quite a beating since Ricks original paint job and has been resprayed.

Mike Hinkle
(The Formally Unknown Mechanic)

I had heard stories of a mechanic in the area that sounded too unlikely to believe. Tall tales of a "Mechanics" mechanic. A man that other auto repair shop owners go to when they are stumped. With some vague verbal directions whispered in a hushed voice I set out on a quest to find this man and enroll him in the Big Banana Car project. After a winding twisting journey through the roads of Pennsylvania I found myself standing before the gate to his kingdom. However, it was after 5pm on a Friday and he had gone home for the weekend. With a tear in my eye I turned and left, vowing to return on Monday. I went back bright and early and outlined the big banana car build and my particular needs. I then stood back as he pondered my request and nervously awaited his decision. "Sure", he said.

Gene Toner (The Elder)

I needed some Fiero seats and had been driving past a house that had a couple of Fiero's in the yard. I stopped to inquire about them having no notion that the home owner was such a huge car nut.

We got chatting about the big banana car and Gene was hooked.

Gene Toner (The Younger)

Gene is a very skilled auto mechanic and sees solutions before I have even noticed the problem.

I like to say that Gene and his dad are my favourite pair of Genes.

Banana Car FAQ

Why did you build a banana car?
I have built many hotrods over the years and I wanted to do something completely different and, dare I say it, ridiculous. I couldn't think of anything more different and ridiculous than driving around in a banana.
Although there was a time when living in Flint Michigan that my only car was a 1930 Model A Ford hotrod. It was my daily driver for 3 - 1/2 years.

What is it's top speed?
Well, I have had it up to 85 but I hasten to add that was in Texas where the speed limit was 80 so I was only doing 5 over. However, I was still the slowest one on the road.

What do you do when it rains?
I get wet! Sometimes really, really wet!! It's like a motorcycle in that way. You just have to accept that there will be times when you encounter rain.
I do pop an umbrella at stop lights but as soon as I start driving it flips inside out

What is it made of?
I took a 1993 Ford pick up truck and took off the cab, bed and hood. I then made the skeleton shape of a banana out of metal, covered that in chicken wire, sprayed it with foam, sculpted the foam to a nice banana shape and then put fibreglass over the top.
It took a weekend.
Just kidding. It took about 2 1/2 years but that was working mostly on weekends.

Where was it made?
I started building the banana car in Monclova Ohio and Bowling Green Ohio. I then moved everything to Quakertown Pennsylvania and finished the build in Coopersburg Pennsylvania.

Do you trailer it from state to state?
No. I drive it.

How many Miles Per Gallon does it get?
It has a 302 ci V8 engine and gets about 14 to 15 miles per gallon which is probably the same as the original F-150.

Before

A 1993 Ford F-150 Pick up truck

After

The Big Banana Car

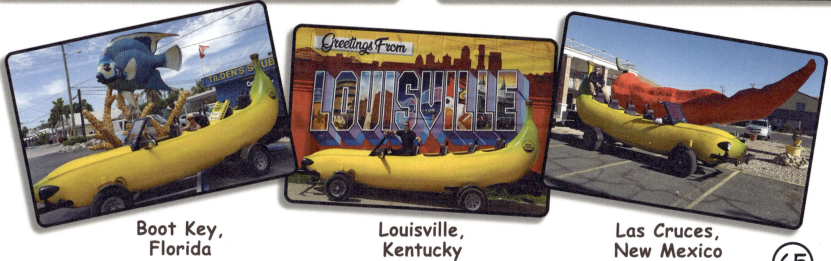

Boot Key,
Florida

Louisville,
Kentucky

Las Cruces,
New Mexico

Ordering Information:
To purchase individual copies of this book visit **BigBananaCar.com/book**

Special discounts are available on quantity purchases by corporations, associations, and others including orders by U.S. bookstores and wholesalers.
Please contact Steve Braithwaite: *Steve@BigBananaCar.com*

The Mutant Press

Printed in the United States of America